A
Portrait
of
Wirral's Railways

A Portrait of Wirral's Railways

by

Roger Jermy, MA, Dip.Ed, CBiol, MIBiol

CONTENTS

First published 1987 by Countyvise Ltd., 1 & 3 Grove Road, Rock Ferry, Birkenhead L42 3XS.
ISBN 0 907768 17 2

and

Avon AngliA Publications & Services, Annesley House, 21 Southside, Weston-super-Mare, Avon BS23 2QU.
ISBN 0 905466 78 X

Copyright © Roger Jermy, MA, Dip.Ed, CBiol, MIBiol, 1987.
Photoset and printed by Birkenhead Press Ltd., 1 & 3 Grove Road, Rock Ferry, Birkenhead L42 3XS.

FOREWORD

From the days of the horse-drawn tramroads to the present day diesel and electric era Wirral has been an area of railway interest. Although largely lacking in spectacular scenic backdrops and major engineering features such as tunnels and viaducts it has exhibited a huge variety of activities from heavy freight trains to intensive commuter services, from the hubbub of dockland to the tranquility of the rural branch line.

Recently both groups and individuals have researched and published individual line histories and have detailed their locomotives, operations and services. This volume does not set out to duplicate these works; instead it attempts to portray some of the variety and uniqueness of Wirral's railways, including just sufficient historical detail to place the picture in context. A selection of the more specialised works may be found in the bibliography.

The majority of photographs in the book has not been previously published. I would like to thank all of the photographers and copyright holders who have so kindly agreed to make their material available.

Roger Jermy
Stroud,
Gloucestershire.
1987

Wirral's Railways: The Background

'Twixt Mersey and Dee' lies Wirral. Today much of the peninsula lies within the Metropolitan County of Merseyside, but until local government reorganisation in 1974 Wirral formed part of Cheshire. The historic 'Wirral Hundred' included the lands lying to the west of a line drawn from the Stanlow Point on the River Mersey to Blacon (near Chester) and thence to Burton Point on the Dee Estuary.

The pattern of railway development in Wirral has depended upon a combination of geological, geographical and climatic features and the railways in turn have contributed to the pattern of social, economic and industrial development in the area.

The surface landform of Wirral consists of boulder clay together with much alluvium and wind blown sand, especially on the Irish Sea coastline. Thrust upwards through this are sandstones forming the low ridges extending from Bidston and Claughton to Storeton and Clatterbridge in East Wirral, and from West Kirby to Neston and Burton in the west. The River Dee, forming Wirral's western boundary is an old, wide and shallow river. The Mersey to the east is, in contrast, much narrower and deeper at its mouth. Being more suitable for larger vessels it has been responsible for the port developments stretching from Birkenhead to Ellesmere Port from whence the Manchester Ship Canal has allowed sea-going vessels to reach Manchester.

The climate of Wirral is mild in comparison with areas further inland. It has a record of low rainfall and long hours of sunshine thus encouraging the growing of crops. Wirral thus possessed a widespread pattern of farms and settlement. However the early part of the agricultural and industrial revolutions by-passed Wirral and as the 19th century arrived the area was little more than a quiet backwater with few and poorly made roads. The major settlement in the west surrounded the port of Neston-cum-Parkgate, whilst Tranmere was the largest township in the east. It was the rapid development of the Port of Liverpool and the introduction of the first steam ferries across the Mersey in 1817 that initiated Wirral's rapid subsequent changes. Between 1821 and 1841 the population of Birkenhead rose from just 200 to over 8,000. The opening of the Birkenhead Railway contributed to the population reaching some 30,000 by 1850.

Several Wirral sandstone quarries were worked to supply stone for the developing industrial, commercial and dock facilities in Liverpool and Birkenhead. The earliest railways in Wirral were linked with two of these. The first, the $\frac{1}{2}$ mile long Flaybrick Hill Tramway, was opened by 1818. It conveyed stone from a quarry at Flaybrick at the side of Bidston Hill to a quay at Wallasey Pool for onward transport by river barge. The second line, the Storeton Tramway, was $2\frac{1}{2}$ miles long and linked the extensive quarries on Storeton Ridge with the Mersey at Bromborough Pool. It was opened in 1838. These two quarries provided much fine building stone. The Flaybrick line had closed by the 1860s and the lower part of its route disappeared beneath dock development. The Storeton line survived until the advent of the motor lorry caused its demise after 1900. Both of these early lines were horse and gravity worked.

Early Birkenhead industries included William Laird's Iron Works (establishing a local tradition of building iron ships) and Thomas Brassey's works. Ambitious plans were drawn up for dock development. Several plans for railways to Birkenhead were proposed in the 1820s. The first had its origins in 1823. However the

Parliamentary application, made by the Liverpool & Birmingham Railway Company, was rejected in 1824. The application requested powers to build a line from Birkenhead to Birmingham via Chester. A tunnel linking the Birkenhead terminus with Liverpool was contemplated! A second application, made in 1826, was similarly rejected. It was, no doubt, the construction of the Liverpool & Manchester Railway which diverted the attention of the Birkenhead line's promoters to an alternative route for their Birmingham railway. Eventually the Grand Junction Railway was built.

The need for a railway to link Chester with Birkenhead was still appreciated. In 1830 George Stephenson surveyed the countryside between these points and favoured a line running between the Mersey and the more easterly sandstone ridge. An alternative route was drawn up by Francis Giles. This more westerly route would have commenced at Wallasey Pool and scaled the sandstone ridge by means of some severe gradients before heading for Chester. Despite some major engineering problems this scheme received support from some Liverpool parties. However after years of quarrelling and indecision the Stephenson route was favoured and in 1837 the Royal Assent was received for the Act of Incorporation of the Chester & Birkenhead Railway. Services on the single line between Grange Lane, Birkenhead, and Chester began on 23 September 1840. Although the Chester & Crewe Railway trains also ran into Chester the Grand Junction Railway (which owned the latter line) held up passengers by making sure that there were no connections between the two services! An early development from the Chester & Birkenhead was to have been a branch from Bebington via Thornton Hough to the colleries at Neston, though naught came of this scheme.

The continued development of docks and industry stimulated the movement of goods and passengers to and from the centres of Birkenhead and Liverpool (the latter via the efficient ferries). An extension from Grange Lane to the Monks Ferry was opened in 1844 and increasing traffic led to the need for a double line of track and additional stations and facilities.

The increasing importance of Birkenhead is illustrated by the decision of the Great Western Railway (which, together with the London & North Western Railway, had absorbed the interests of the Chester & Birkenhead and its immediate successors) to run through trains between Birkenhead and Paddington. This tradition was to continue for over one hundred years.

The environs of Birkenhead provided much of the housing for the industrial labourers while more fashionable residential developments arose elsewhere, at Neston, Hoylake (where earlier Sir John Stanley had established a hotel) and New Brighton (where Atherton and Agnew, two Liverpool merchants, had bought land to establish a seaside resort). Railways were constructed to link these centres to Birkenhead. The branch from Hooton to Neston and Parkgate was opened in 1866 and was subsequently extended (1886) to make an end-on connection with the Hoylake Railway at West Kirby. The

Chester train leaving Rock Ferry in the 1920s.

importance of Hooton as a railway junction dates from 1863 when a branch to Helsby was opened. This facilitated movement of goods and passengers between Birkenhead and Warrington and Manchester. In 1870 a new connection, built near Helsby, allowed traffic from the Cheshire Lines Railway to gain access to Birkenhead.

It was in 1863 also that Parliamentary powers were granted for the construction of a line to link Seacombe with Hoylake, then still a small village. The line's promoters envisaged opening up the area as a dormitory area for Birkenhead. Constructed by the Hoylake Railway Company it opened in 1866 between Wallasey Bridge Road and Hoylake. Despite the granting of some additional powers financial difficulties prevented branches to New Brighton, West Kirby and Neston being built in the 1860s. After periods of time in various ownership the line was extended to Birkenhead Park (to make an end-on connection with the Mersey Railway), to West Kirby, to Wallasey and New Brighton, and in the 1890s to Seacombe, thus forming the system of the Wirral Railway. New Brighton developed into a popular destination for day trippers from Liverpool, whilst Hoylake and West Kirby developed into quieter and more refined resorts and residential areas!

For some time, however, there had been a pressing need for an improved link between Birkenhead and Liverpool via a rail tunnel. The original Bill for a pneumatic railway was passed in 1866 but it was not until 1886 that the Mersey Railway opened for traffic between James Street in Liverpool and Green Lane in Birkenhead. Steam provided the motive power. Subsequent developments extended the line to beneath the Cheshire Lines Committee station in Liverpool, to Rock Ferry (where the GW/LNW line was joined), and to Birkenhead Park to meet the Wirral lines.

The final main line of rails in Wirral was to pass between the two sandstone ridges and open up the central districts. Early schemes were not realised and it was not until 1889 that construction powers were transferred to the Manchester, Sheffield & Lincolnshire Railway and the Wrexham, Mold & Connah's Quay Railway jointly, allowing the line to be built. These companies were attracted by the prospect of independent access to the port of Birkenhead. The new railway was opened to traffic in 1896 although a proposed branch linking Prenton and Oxton with Birkenhead was not proceeded with. This line became part of the Great Central Railway in 1905.

By 1900 the main rail routes of Wirral were thus established, though extensive private rail systems were to develop in association with the industries of Ellesmere Port, Bromborough, Port Sunlight and Birkenhead's dockland. Various contractors used temporary lines during their construction and after completion the systems provided vital feeder traffic to the main lines. The majority of Wirral's stations had their own sidings serving the needs of local industry and commerce. In the early 1900s the Chester line was quadruple-tracked between Birkenhead and Ledsham as a result of the increasing traffic, and the Mersey Railway was electrified in 1903 making the underground journey to Liverpool easier, quicker, cleaner and quieter. Additional stations were opened for newer residential areas such as Caldy, while Port Sunlight station allowed workmen to reach the nearby soap factory. By 1910 Great Western Railway passenger trains linked Birkenhead's Woodside terminus (opened in 1878) with Paddington, Dover and Bournemouth, and extensive local services operated on all lines.

The 'Grouping' of railways which occurred after the First World War allowed the Great Western Railway to retain its independence. The Wirral Railway and the London & North Western Railway became part of the London Midland & Scottish Railway whilst the Bidston to Hawarden line became part of the London & North

Eastern Railway. The Mersey Railway was excluded from the grouping and remained nominally independent until the railways were nationalised in 1948, although along with all other railways it came under Government control during the Second World War.

Developments took place between the two wars despite the increasing competition from the lorry and the private car. The LMS introduced through coaches between New Brighton and Euston via West Kirby and Hooton, and Port Sunlight became a public rather than a private station. In the 1930s the Wirral Railway was electrified between Park and both West Kirby and New Brighton, permitting through running between Liverpool and the two termini. The lines became increasingly heavily used by evening and weekend excursionists, and further residential development resulted in the opening of Manor Road station in 1938.

During the Second World War the lines of Wirral assumed great strategic importance and as such were the target for much bombing. In the last months of 1940 and in May 1941 Birkenhead in particular received especial treatment and various stations, including Park and North, received direct hits. The dock lines were damaged yet services were maintained. Traffic on the Mersey and Wirral lines continued despite some trainsets being destroyed and over half the rolling stock receiving some damage! The heroic exploits of some Wirral railwaymen during this period have been recorded elsewhere and have been justly rewarded.

After the war increasing private car ownership brought pressure upon the more lightly used stations and services. The electrification of the Wirral lines shortened the journey times on the direct West Kirby to Liverpool line and made the roundabout route via Hooton and Neston less attractive. The stations at Caldy and Thurstaston were closed in 1954 and the remainder of the line succumbed two years later, though a goods service survived for a few more years. The Seacombe branch was also under pressure and it too lost its passenger service in 1960 with the goods service lingering on for three more years. Further closures occurred on the Birkenhead and Chester line. Birkenhead Town had long been unnecessary and it closed in 1945. Both Ledsham and Mollington were away from population centres and these too were closed. Similar reasons caused the closure of Storeton and Burton Point on the former LNER line.

The electrification of the London Midland Region's West Coast Main Line in the 1960s and the reduction in the length of the Euston Station platforms caused the disappearance of the through Birkenhead to Euston carriages. At the same time the through Paddington to Birkenhead services ceased, as did the services to Shrewsbury and mid-Wales. Steam hauled suburban services had given way to multiple unit trains on the non-electrified lines in the early 1960s yet Birkenhead was one of the last active areas of steam locomotives in the country. The late '60s saw an accelerating run-down of freight services. The once familiar cattle train became but a memory and many firms switched from rail to road collection and delivery. Such service reductions demanded track rationalisation and both sidings and main lines received attention. 1969 saw the Birkenhead to Chester line revert to being double tracked; several station platforms became redundant and stations became unstaffed, with inevitable increase in vandalism and an increasing air of desolation. The closure of the John Summers (later BSC) steel works at Shotton resulted in the cessation of the Bidston Dock to Shotwick Sidings ore trains which all but eliminated freight traffic from the mid-Wirral line. The principle source of freight traffic on the Helsby and Chester lines became the oil traffic to refineries at Stanlow, although some grain and coal trains continued to use Birkenhead Docks. Over much of the Wirral it is now possible to spend several hours at the lineside and see nothing else but multiple unit diesel or electric trains. Times have changed!

A
Portrait
of
Wirral's Railways
The Early Years

Early railway scenes at Ellesmere Port showing, below, the hotel and station and, right, an LNWR 0-6-0 standing in the platform. Quite why the demure young ladies and nine railwaymen should be posing with a goods train is not clear.

The picture on the previous page shows an LNWR 4-4-0 speeding through Port Sunlight in the 1920s.

HOTEL & STATION, ELLESMERE PORT.

The West Kirby branch originally terminated at Neston & Parkgate but was extended to West Kirby with services traversing the entire length of the line in 1886. This scene dates from that year and shows a Hooton train waiting to leave West Kirby. Note the range of railway ancillary equipment, signal box and signals, turntable, water crane and points rodding.

The earliest known photograph of Hoylake terminus shows what is believed to be Ashton, a 2-2-2T and one of the earliest locomotives to be used on the line. The cramped 4-wheeled coaches running on poor track must have provided a rough ride for the few passengers that the original company carried in its brief and impecunious history.

Gosport, *a K class Manning Wardle, spent a brief period in the early 1900s hauling loads of sandstone from the Storeton Hill Quarries to Port Sunlight for use in works associated with the quadrupling of the Rock Ferry to Ledsham Junction line. Owned at the time by Price & Reeves, Contractors, it later found use on dock building jobs and in a Yorkshire colliery. It is shown here at Storeton.*

Wirral Railway 4-4-2T No. 1 awaits departure from Birkenhead North with a westbound train shortly before the line was incorporated into the London, Midland & Scottish Railway. The ground signal is of a Wirral Railway type. The 'Wirral Horn' symbol is still visible in the masonry of North Station.

In 1902 Lever Bros chartered four trains to take their employees to a Paris Exhibition via Crewe, Kensington (Addison Road) and Dover. The one seen here is headed by two well turned out GWR locomotives, a 4-4-0 and an 0-6-0.

Wirral Railway 4-4-2T No. 4 at the head of a motley train of which the leading vehicle is a six-wheeler with two four-wheelers following. A loading gauge is just visible on the right.

Drifting steam obscures the coaching stock as a Great Western 2-4-0T enters Heswall station in the early years of the century to collect a very modest number of passengers.

The recently-arrived Wirral Railway train has stopped short of the points in this view of New Brighton. It can then draw down and run round its train via the engine release road.

Before the building of the Woodside terminus, trains ran to Monks Ferry station which later became a coaling point for steam tugs. The upper view shows the Monks Ferry site looking towards the Mersey. In contrast, the lower view shows the distinctive and pleasing architecture of the station buildings at Spital around 1900.

The Birkenhead to Chester Line

The ultimate terminus of the Birkenhead Joint line was at Woodside, close to the banks of the Mersey and the major ferry to Liverpool. The 5-platform station was well appointed with a taxi road, refreshment rooms, large concourse and impressive overall arched roof. Between the platform lines were loops for freeing locomotives from their trains and sidings for the temporary stabling of coaching stock. In former years a small turntable and locomotive sidings were present close to the station throat. On leaving the platform trains plunged into a dark winding tunnel beneath the Birkenhead streets before emerging into murky daylight at Town station close by the original 1840s Grange Lane terminus. The tunnel leading to the Monks Ferry diverged at this point. Between Town and Rock Ferry there was formerly a constant hubbub of railway activity with the sounds of shunting in the extensive carriage sidings and coal yards, the heavy trains rumbling onto the Docks link and the clamour and dust of the locomotive depots. Today the coal sidings have disappeared and the dock traffic is considerably reduced. The carriage sidings have long since been lifted and even the locomotive depot has succumbed to persistent closure threats.

Approaching Rock Ferry the line overlooks the industrial Mersey margins yet beyond it passes through suburbia including the still-attractive village of Port Sunlight, sadly bereft of its elm trees. Today only the parkland to the west of the line between Spital and Bromborough has defied the spread of the housing estates. Hooton, the present day terminus of the Merseyrail electric trains, was in former years a busy

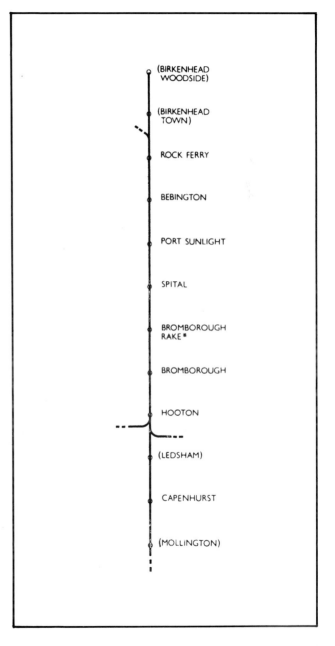

(BIRKENHEAD
WOODSIDE)

(BIRKENHEAD
TOWN)

ROCK FERRY

BEBINGTON

PORT SUNLIGHT

SPITAL

BROMBOROUGH
RAKE *

BROMBOROUGH

HOOTON

(LEDSHAM)

CAPENHURST

(MOLLINGTON)

Stanier 2-6-4T 42616 heads the 3.25pm Birkenhead to Chester past Blackpool Street signal box in May 1966. The dock lines are to the left.

junction. Here is the boundary between the suburban sprawl and the typical Cheshire farmland which can be seen from diesel trains as they provide the continuation of the service to Chester. The ugly towers of the Nuclear Fuels plant at Capenhurst are unwelcome intruders into this pleasing, if unspectacular, landscape. Shortly after the site of the former Mollington station the line leaves Wirral crossing the Shropshire Union canal on an impressive sandstone viaduct.

Being for much of its life a joint line the Birkenhead to Chester exhibited a wide diversity of locomotives and rolling stock. In early years London & North Western and Great Western Railway types predominated, though later, stock from other pre-grouping companies and LMS 'standard' types appeared. Occasional visitors from the LNER arrived via the link from the Cheshire Lines Railway at Helsby and Southern stock appeared regularly on the through trains linking Wirral with the south coast resorts. Nationalisation brought many British Railways-built locomotives and coaches to the line.

For many years services included long distance passenger trains, sometimes with refreshment facilities, which were timetabled to stop at Rock Ferry and Hooton. In addition there were ample stopping passenger services with some trains being of the rail motor or push-pull type. Long distance freight trains carried imported meat, grain and perishables traffic to London, and linked Birkenhead Docks with Bristol, Birmingham, Carlisle and Yorkshire. Local freight services ferried wagonload traffic between the various yards and private sidings on the line. In steam days locomotives were supplied and serviced by the depots at Mollington Street (Birkenhead) and Chester. There were many visitors from London, Wales, the Midlands and the western half of England. Freight vehicles included specialist wagons for conveying cattle, grain and heavy engineering items as well as the ubiquitous open wagons and covered vans. Various local private owner wagons and containers brightened up the scene, including those of the Wirral Colliery Company and the Monks Ferry Steam Coal Company.

After the demise of steam, 2- or 4-car multiple unit diesel trains fulfilled the passenger requirements, mostly calling at all stations between Rock Ferry and Chester. With the exception of some summer excursions the majority of through trains ceased in the 1960s. The less frequent freight trains became entrusted to diesel locomotives, standard types in their workstained liveries.

Station architecture and facilities, never outstanding, became quite depressing, with the formerly attractive station gardens becoming largely untended. At some stations, such as Capenhurst, passenger accommodation is now entirely lacking whilst at others, such as Bebington, bus-stop type shelters have been provided following demolition of the former brick buildings. The 'unmanned station' experiment at Spital resulted in the unwelcome attention of the vandal and graffiti artist. Extensive and expensive repairs were necessary before the electrified services were extended. The reinstatement of station staff has allowed better standards to be maintained. Only at Hooton and Rock Ferry do facilities approach those of former years although even at these stations they are somewhat restricted. Of the peninsula's most grand station, Woodside, only the side walls remain, the concourse, taxi-road and platforms being given over to car parking. The overall roof was demolished soon after closure, the wrongly placed and almost unused main entrance was

GW Prairie tank 5103 of Chester (West) depot appears below between Bromborough and Spital with a stopping train of mixed stock in May 1958. In contrast, the powerful 9F 2-10-0 92234 heads a SLS special train on the Chester line in the picture on the right.

A busy 1958 day on the 'Joint' line; 42977 heads a Chester train past Green Lane Junction, while 6346 waits with a rake of goods and mineral wagons and a pannier tank shunts the sidings.

knocked down, and the hole-in-the-wall side entrance relegated to providing car park access.

The present third-rail electrification, as well as necessitating some platform lengthening and alterations, has had the effect of splitting the line into two parts, a northerly section with a more frequent service of multiple units calling at an increased number of stations, and a southerly section between Hooton and Chester served by diesel trains. On both parts of the line colour light signals have replaced the former semaphore arms, various boxes have been closed (such as at Bebington and Spital) and

redundant buildings and parts of the trackbed have been offered for sale. Multiple aspect colour light signals have replaced the former semaphore arms. The 'healing hand of nature' is covering over some of the former yards and sidings.

BIRKENHEAD TO CHESTER

1837 12 Jul Chester & Birkenhead Railway Act passed.
1840 23 Sep Line opened from Chester to Birkenhead (Grange Lane). Intermediate stations at

In 1955 a 41XX Prairie tank is replenished at Birkenhead locomotive depot despite the construction work on new coaling facilities. Ten of these tanks were shedded at Birkenhead for use on stopping trains.

		Bebington, Hooton, Sutton and Mollington.
1844	23 Oct	Extension to Monks Ferry opened.
1846	Jun	Stations at Lime Kiln Lane (became Tranmere in 1853, closed in 1857) and Rock Lane (closed 1862).
	26 Jun	Birkenhead, Lancashire & Cheshire Junction Railway formed.
1847	5 Apr	Grange Lane to Cathcart Street goods line opened (for Birkenhead Docks).
	22 Jul	Birkenhead, Lancashire & Cheshire Junction Railway and Chester & Birkenhead Railway amalgamated. Line double-tracked.
1855	18 Aug	Great Western Railway opened goods shed at Cathcart Street.
1857	1 May	Great Western Railway started to run Birkenhead to Birmingham trains.
1859	1 Aug	Line became Birkenhead Railway.
1860	20 Nov	Birkenhead Railway absorbed jointly by the Great Western and London & North Western Railways.
1861	1 Oct	Great Western Railway commenced through Birkenhead to Paddington trains.
1862	31 Oct	Rock Ferry station opened.
1863	Jul	Sutton became Ledsham.
	Dec	Tranmere Pool Branch (goods) opened.

1878	1 Apr	Green Lane Junction to Birkenhead (Woodside) opened. Monks Ferry station closed to passengers.
1891	15 Jun	Mersey Railway link opened at Rock Ferry.
1892	7 Mar	Paddington to Birkenhead trains started to include corridor coaches.
1894		Great Western Railway operated through services from Liverpool to Paddington via Mersey Railway.
1900-1905		Line quadrupled from Birkenhead Grange Lane to Ledsham Junction.
1914	Mar	Port Sunlight station opened for workmen.
1927	9 May	Port Sunlight opened for public use.
1945	7 May	Birkenhead Town station closed.
1959	20 Jul	Ledsham station closed.
1960	7 Mar	Mollington station closed for passengers (for goods 4 Jan 1965).
1967	6 Nov	Birkenhead Woodside station closed.
1969		Former fast lines lifted between Rock Ferry and Hooton; slow lines lifted between Ledsham Junction and Hooton. Line became double-tracked.
1983		Preliminary electrification work commenced between Rock Ferry and Hooton.
1984		Construction of Bromborough Rake station commenced.
1985		Third rail electrification extended from Rock Ferry to Hooton. Electric services commenced.

In the upper illustration a Rock Ferry dmu pauses at Capenhurst where the platforms and footbridge have been daubed with paint messages. The contrasting freight scene in the centre pictures a train of oil tanks from Stanlow in charge of a pair of class 25s which will have run round their train at Hooton. In the lower picture D234 prepares to leave platform 2 at Woodside with the midday Paddington train on 12 February 1967.

The Helsby Branch

The branch between Hooton and Helsby includes the longest length of dead straight track on the west side of Great Britain. On leaving Hooton the line passes through typical Wirral wooded countryside before reaching Little Sutton and Ellesmere Port. Originally villages, they now have been linked into an anonymous sprawl of semi-detached suburbia, a dormitory for the extensive industrial sites which have been developed along the sides of the Manchester Ship Canal and the Mersey. As the line leaves the former Wirral Hundred, between Ellesmere Port and Stanlow, the once extensive views over the low-lying marshes have been replaced by a skyline of cooling towers and refinery flares.

Although the line was constructed largely for freight traffic, substantial passenger stations were provided, and from a distance at least, those at Little Sutton and Ellesmere Port retain something of their former splendour. The sandstone buildings, resistant to much of the local air pollution, remain although most of the platform fittings and furniture have been removed. The passenger traffic at Ellesmere Port even warrants the retention of a taxi rank and a small refreshment bar survives in the station forecourt. One must, however, possess the right key to gain access to the station 'Gents'; even its sign has long since disappeared!

The passenger traffic, always largely of a local nature, now consists of a two-car multiple unit shuttling between Hooton and Helsby with only occasional trains proceeding beyond these points. Freight trains, formerly of wide diversity of type, origin and destination, now consist of rakes of oil tankers hauled by class 47 and 25

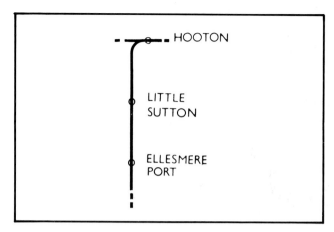

diesel locomotives to and from the refineries. These provide sharp contrast to the variety of locomotives of LMS, LNER and Great Western types which formerly provided the motive power!

HOOTON TO HELSBY

1863	1 Jul	Line opened between Hooton and Helsby. Intermediate stations at Sutton, Whitby Locks and Ince (later Ince & Elton).
1869	1 Sep	Link to CLC at West Cheshire Junction (Helsby) opened. CLC trains use running powers to gain access to Birkenhead (CLC Shore Road goods depot opened 1 Jul 1871).
1870		Whitby Locks became Ellesmere Port station.
1886		Sutton became Little Sutton station.
1940	23 Oct	Stanlow & Thornton station opened for workmen.
1941	24 Feb	Stanlow & Thornton station opened to public.

The West Kirby Branch

From its junction with the Chester & Birkenhead line at Hooton the branch curved sharply away to the west, heading through rural tranquility and leafy cuttings towards the township of Neston with Parkgate. From Parkgate onward the line followed the coastline of the Dee estuary, with the small stations and their sidings located to the seaward side of the villages they served. West Kirby was the passenger terminus although a sharply curved spur allowed passage of some trains onto the lines of the Wirral Railway. This link was principally used for goods trains although from time to time passenger trains were scheduled to use it.

The trackbed of much of the line has been converted into the Wirral Way, the first 'country park' in Great Britain. Cheshire County Council was prompted to provide the finance and the organisation to transform what was formerly a 'derelict industrial site' into a well-signposted public walkway and bridleway. A visitor centre has been established at Thurstaston, but the present pride of the line is the beautifully restored station at Hadlow Road, Willaston. Track has been relaid past the platform, a signalbox has been erected and even items such as station signs and strategically placed luggage have been added. The station, with its restored interior is a 'must' for all visitors to Wirral. Mercifully the vandals have seen fit to leave the station alone.

No other station buildings survive along the route although two station houses, at Heswall and Parkgate, and a row of railway cottages at Heswall are in private ownership. Various bridges remain although others have been demolished.

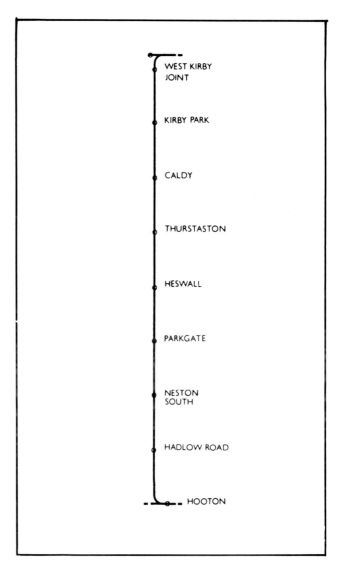

The upper picture on the opposite page is of a Helsby-bound train passing Whitby, and the lower one of a Class 47 hauling a coal train through Childer Thornton, both in November 1985.

In its heyday the branch was the preserve of small engine types with Great Western open-cabbed 6-wheeled tanks and LNWR coal tanks hauling the trains. Later track improvements allowed larger 2-6-2 tanks to appear and in the line's final years locomotives as large as the 'Crab' 2-6-0's, Stanier 8F's and Fairburn 2-6-4 tanks worked the freight services. Non-corridor stock was the rule on most passenger trains. Regular, but somewhat unusual, visitors to the line were the electric multiple units of Wirral lines which traversed the branch en route to and from Horwich for overhaul.

HOOTON TO WEST KIRBY

1862	17 Jul	Birkenhead Joint Act passed, for a branch from Hooton to Parkgate.
1866	1 Oct	Line opened. Intermediate stations at Hadlow Road (near Willaston) and Neston.
1882	12 Jul	Act for West Kirby Extension passed.
1886	19 Apr	Parkgate to West Kirby extension opened. New stations at Parkgate, Heswall and Thurstaston opened and Parkgate old station closed.
1894	Oct	Kirby Park station opened.
1909	May	Caldy station opened.
1954	1 Feb	Thurstaston and Caldy stations closed.
	5 Jul	Kirby Park station closed.
1956	17 Sep	Line closed to passengers.
1962	7 May	Line closed to goods.
1969		Cheshire County Council purchased trackbed to form the Wirral Way Country Park.

The Hooton-West Kirby line might have survived if a diesel shuttle had replaced the steam hauled trains but the upper and lower scenes opposite are only driver training for the Chester line. At the top the station is Heswall and at the bottom Parkgate. The centre scene shows a Stanier 2-6-2T running round its train at West Kirby. Bridge strengthening and some relaxation in axle loading restrictions allowed larger locomotives on the branch in later years.

On this page Hadlow Road station is shown, firstly, in 'Joint' line days with a train arriving from Hooton and, secondly, in 1984 after its restoration by the Wirral Country Park Authority. Track has been laid between the platforms, a signal box has been erected and the station buildings have been restored and re-equipped. Items of luggage and enamel advertisements add the final touches to a skilful piece of restoration and preservation.

The Mid-Wirral Line

This was the last of the main lines to appear in the Wirral landscape. It had its origins in the attempts of the Manchester, Sheffield & Lincolnshire, and Wrexham, Mold & Connah's Quay Railways to obtain an alternative means of access to the docks at Birkenhead. After opening it became the most westerly extremity of the Great Central and later the London & North Eastern Railways. Whilst handling considerable freight traffic its passenger potential was somewhat limited and not helped by the inconvenient siting of some of its stations, Storeton, Heswall Hills and Burton Point being such examples. However an extensive stopping train service linked both Chester (Northgate) and Wrexham with North Wirral. Trains passed over the triangular junctions of the Wirral Railway at Bidston to gain access to the Seacombe branch terminus (actually belonging to the Wirral concern).

Trains enter the Wirral Hundred close to Burton Point station where there are views across the upper Dee estuary towards North Wales. Passing inland through sandstone cuttings the trains reach Neston where the Hooton to West Kirby line passed beneath. Embankments, cuttings and yet more embankments allow the line to descend through Heswall Hills and Storeton towards Upton where the valley floor is followed until Bidston is reached and the line joins Wirral Railway metals. The approach to Seacombe, also through sandstone cuttings, now forms the second Mersey Tunnel approach.

The Great Central Railway built sidings and a locomotive depot at Bidston which survived until the

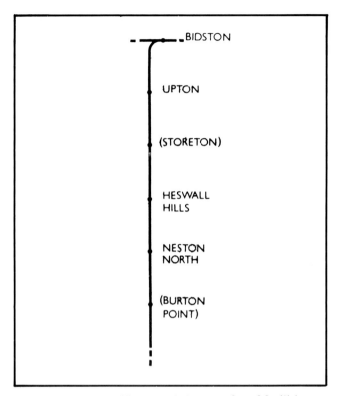

decline of dock traffic caused the transfer of facilities to Birkenhead (Mollington Street). Former Great Central and LNER locomotive types were common on the line until British Railways and ex-LMS standard types took over in the late 1950s. Well remembered are the heavy trains, hauled by the massive 9F 2-10-0s which noisily fought their way up Storeton Bank, 'neath pillars of smoke', conveying iron ore from Bidston Dock to the Shotwick Sidings of the John Summers steelworks.

Today the line is bereft of freight traffic and two-car diesel units ply back and forth between Bidston and Wrexham with the passenger service. Plans for steam hauled excursions on the line have not been realised and the line's stations, with reduced facilities, face an uncertain future.

BIDSTON TO HAWARDEN BRIDGE

1883 13 Jan Powers of Wirral Railway incorporated by Certificate.

1885 31 Dec Construction authorised; not commenced.

1888 Prenton and Oxton Branch authorised; plans abandoned 1890.

1889 12 Aug Wirral Railway powers transferred to the Manchester, Sheffield & Lincolnshire Railway and Wrexham, Mold & Connah's Quay Railway (Wirral Railways Committee).

1895 6 Jul Line became the Dee & Birkenhead Railway.

1896 16 Mar Line opened for goods.

18 May Line opened for passengers. Intermediate stations at Neston (later Neston & Parkgate, then Neston North), Barnston (later Storeton for Barnston) and Upton.

7 Jul Named North Wales & Liverpool Railway.

1898 1 May Heswall Hills station opened.

1899 1 Aug Burton Point station opened.

1905 1 Jan Line became part of the Great Central Railway.

1923 1 Jan Line became part of the London & Northern Eastern Railway.

1948 1 Jan Line became part of British Railways.

1951 3 Dec Storeton station closed for passengers (for goods 3 February 1964).

1955 5 Dec Burton Point station closed.

Class 9F 92047 returns a rake of Summers ore hoppers to Bidston Dock in 1965.

Just two minutes turn-round time were sufficient for this two car unit at Bidston. Visits of the Wrexham stopping trains have to be fitted into the gaps in the West Kirby-Bidston-Liverpool electric service.

Stanier Class 3 2-6-2T No. 40080 pauses at Neston with a stopping train from Seacombe to Wrexham. Originally this station was known as Neston & Parkgate, later as Neston North and then plain Neston after the closure of the near-by platform on the West Kirby-Hooton line.

A
Portrait
of
Wirral's Railways
Steam Heyday

AN UNMISTAKABLE MERSEY RAILWAY LOCOMOTIVE

*Steam locomotives working below ground had a style all of their own.
This shows well in this view of Mersey Railway 0-6-4T No. 7 Liverpool
standing in the middle road at Rock Ferry.*

*On the previous page a 'Dean Goods' 0-6-0 storms through Hooton
with a mixed goods train in the mid 1950s. One of these locomotives is
preserved in Swindon Railway Museum.*

PERIOD RAILWAY SCENE AT WEST KIRBY

All the elements of railways past appear in this view of West Kirby including signal box, signals, wires and rodding, water tank and water crane and goods and passenger rolling stock.

The interior of Birkenhead (Docks) locomotive shed in the 1930s.

Birkenhead loco depot with steam still outnumbering diesels in 1967.

Two Manchester Ship Canal locomotives stand outside the former LNWR shed at Ellesmere Port.

48157 and 73136 at Mollington Street awaiting their next duties.

35

Freight workings. On the opposite page a pannier tank and its mixed load pass through a gas-lit Ledsham. Here GWR No. 7207 transfers from fast to slow lines at Rock Ferry as it nears its Birkenhead Docks destination and, below, one of the docks locomotives shedded at Birkenhead.

A GWR 2-6-0 with a Chester train at Rock Ferry, right, and taken from the same spot as the picture on page 6. Below, 40080 still carries LMS lettering in the 1950s as it stands at Seacombe & Egremont with a Wrexham train. In the background can be seen the roof of the Seacombe Ferry Terminal.

The former Cambrian Railways inspection saloon is hauled round the curve between Bidston and Upton stations. Although this picture was taken after the 1923 'Grouping' the locomotive, LNWR 7583, still sports its original livery.

Above, Ivatt 2-6-0 No. 46472 pauses for a photographic stop at Thurstaston with a RC & TS Railtour on 26 March 1960. On the right No. 6990 Witherslack Hall, *now preserved, is seen waiting to work the 7.45 Paddington goods as an 8F takes water.*

No. 42942 receives its finishing touches at Birkenhead Mollington Street depot prior to working 1T66 the following day. A gang of Birkenhead's unofficial cleaners are at work.

Close to Meols station is the imposing Station Hotel, its sign recalling traditional links between railways and refreshment for their users. Below, 42942 enters Bebington with a Birkenhead-Llandudno holiday train in 1966, deputising for a 'failed' Black Five!

The Wirral Lines

The Wirral lines have their origins in the Hoylake Railway, an early attempt to link Birkenhead with the Wirral coast. Its poor facilities and badly sited stations produced inevitable failure. It was not until the formation of the Wirral Railway Company that the necessary finance was available to extend and develop the system. The original terminus at Birkenhead Docks, always inconveniently situated, was closed and the line was extended to form an end-on link with the Mersey Railway at Park Station. A triangular junction at Bidston provided connections with the new line to Wallasey and later New Brighton and a second triangle linked this line to the Seacombe branch. The original Hoylake line was double tracked and frequent steam passenger services linked the various termini. The freight traffic was, as might be expected, minimal. Locomotive and stock servicing facilities were established at the site of the former Dock station.

Between Park and North stations the line lies in cutting with the aspect not becoming open until the flat expanse of Bidston Moss is reached. This former ill-drained marshy area, suitable only for grazing sheep, has now been transformed into a complex of motorways and industrial estates. Bidston station, despite somewhat rudimentary facilities, provided (and still provides) an important point of interchange between the Wirral lines and the Mid-Wirral line to Neston and beyond. Beyond Bidston the view from the train was originally over more low-lying farmland but now light industry, gardens and the backs of houses predominate as the settlements, stimulated by the line's existence, steadily grow and merge. Today the lineside area is a large dormitory for the Merseyside business centre. Trains still run into a two-platform terminus at West Kirby which also includes provision for the stabling of empty trains. The sites of the nineteenth century terminus, the coal yard and the link with the Hooton line have disappeared beneath modern developments.

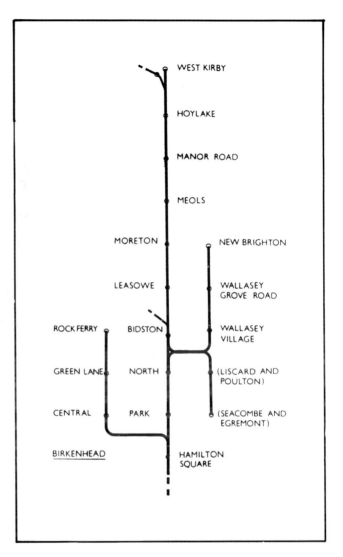

43

Wallasey station, Wirral Railway.

The New Brighton branch has similarly encouraged the development of Wallasey as a residential area. New Brighton station, approached via a long sandstone cutting has a similar two-platform terminus to West Kirby.

The original Wirral locomotives and coaches were replaced largely by former LNWR and LMS standard types until electrification arrived in the 1930s. Since then electric units have provided a rapid through service to Liverpool. For a short time, following the closure of the Seacombe branch, Wrexham and Chester (Northgate) trains were diverted to New Brighton. This brought a service of diesel units to the Wirral lines and even, on the occasions of stock shortages, steam locomotive hauled trains! Thus at the close of the steam era former Great Western Railway pannier tanks from Wrexham (Croes Newydd) shed found their way to the New Brighton terminus, much to the delight of the local railway enthusiast fraternity! Today locomotive hauled trains are confined to engineers' specials.

WIRRAL RAILWAY

1863	28 Jul	Hoylake Railway Company Act passed.
1865	5 Jul	New Brighton Extension Act passed — lapsed.
1866	18 Jan	Line declared open between Docks (Birkenhead) and Hoylake.
	2 Jul	Regular service commenced between Docks and Hoylake. Intermediate stations at Bidston, Moreton and Meols.
	16 Jul	Parkgate Extension Act passed — lapsed.
1870	8 Jul	Line closed by bailiffs until 31 July 1872.
1872	18 Jul	Hoylake & Birkenhead Rail & Tramway Company formed.
1878	1 Apr	Docks station closed; replaced by new Birkenhead North station. Hoylake to West Kirby extension opened.
1881	18 Jun	Seacombe, Hoylake & Deeside Railway formed.

1883	13 Jun	Wirral Railway Company Act passed.
1884	14 Aug	New Brighton Line Act passed.
1888	2 Jan	Extension from Birkenhead North to Park and extension to Grove Road, Wallasey opened.
	30 Mar	Extension from Wallasey to New Brighton opened.
1890	Jun	Bidston station closed until May 1896
1891	11 Jun	Wirral Railway and Seacombe, Hoylake & Deeside amalgamated to form the Wirral Railway Company.
1894		Leasowe station opened.
1895	1 Jun	Seacombe Branch opened. Line to Hoylake double tracked.
1896		Hoylake to West Kirby double tracked. New station built at West Kirby.
1900		First plan to electrify the line — abandoned.
1907		Leasowe Road station opened (later Wallasey Village).
1911		Seacombe to New Brighton trains withdrawn; Seacombe East to North chord closed.
1916	1 Oct	Warren station closed.
1923	1 Jan	Wirral Railway became part of the London, Midland & Scottish Railway.
	Oct	New Brighton to London (Euston) service started.
1935		Electrification scheme commenced.
1938	14 Mar	Electrified service started; also through running between Mersey and Wirral lines. Manor Road station opened.
1948	1 Jan	Line became part of British Railways.
1960	4 Jan	Seacombe Branch closed to passengers.
1963	17 Jun	Seacombe Branch closed to goods

SEACOMBE BRANCH

1895	1 Jan	Branch from Bidston to Seacombe and Egremont opened. Intermediate station at Liscard & Poulton.
1896	18 May	Trains of Dee & Birkenhead Committee (former MS&L and WM&CQ Railways) commenced running over branch.
1960	4 Jan	Seacombe Branch closed to passengers.
1963	17 Jun	Seacombe Branch closed to goods.
1971		Trackbed used for approach to Kingsway (second Mersey road tunnel).

The Wirral Railway's 'Docks' loco shed.

1937 and 1984 views of West Kirby terminus. In the former, the sharp curve to the 'Joint' station is on the left and in the centre, amidst the sidings, is the site of the original Seacombe, Hoylake & Deeside platform, now covered by a bus station.

The Mersey Lines

The Mersey Railway was designed and built as a commuter rail link between Liverpool and the Wirral suburbs. Apart from short-lived experiments, its trains have been confined to the rails of the Mersey and Wirral systems.

From the mid-point of the tunnel beneath the Mersey, the original steam-hauled trains, with their powerful Beyer-Peacock built locomotives, faced a steep uphill climb to their first Wirral stop at Hamilton Square. This underground twin-platform station was the junction where the routes to Park and Rock Ferry diverged. The former of these two branches emerged into daylight at Park and made an end-on connection with the Wirral Railway providing connections to West Kirby and New Brighton. Eventually through running between the two systems took place. The Rock Ferry line passed beneath the Birkenhead streets, emerging briefly into daylight at Central Station, where the offices and depots of the Mersey Railway Company were located. A sharp curve brought the line to Green Lane station, convenient for the shipyards, before trains emerged from the tunnel to run parallel with the Joint line into Rock Ferry station. Here two platforms accommodated Mersey trains.

Electrification occurred at the turn of the century and the disappearance of the sulphurous fumes and the arrival of distinctly American-styled and comfortable rolling stock of multiple unit type caused an upsurge in traffic. The steam locomotives and stock were eventually sold. Once the lines of the Wirral Railways were electrified in the late 1930s through electric train services between the two systems became possible, although on weekdays at least the steel-bodied LMS-built Wirral units rarely appeared on the Rock Ferry line.

The essence of the Mersey Railway's location and function – the 'Most Expeditious Route between Lancashire and Cheshire' – captured by these examples of its publicity.

The 1970s saw the construction of the Liverpool Loop and the flying junction at Hamilton Square. This eliminated the need for train reversal in Liverpool and avoided conflicting train movements, with their inevitable delays, at the busy Hamilton Square junction. Redundant, yet very modern, rolling stock has found its way from British Rail's Southern electrified network to the Mersey and Wirral section.

Now the 'third rail' network has been extended southwards and stations between Rock Ferry and Hooton can receive the benefits of more speedy and frequent through services to Liverpool. The scheme has involved the provision of extended platforms, new sleepering, new stations and altered track layouts.

MERSEY RAILWAY

1866	28 Jun	Mersey Pneumatic Railway Act passed.
1868	31 Jun	Mersey Railway formed.
1871		Mersey Railway Act passed, with orthodox rather then pneumatic operation.
1882		Act passed to extend line beneath Liverpool's CLC station.
1884	17 Jan	Tunnel 'breakthrough' achieved.
1886	20 Jan	Railway opened by the Prince of Wales.
	1 Feb	Railway opened for public use between James Street (Liverpool) and Green Lane (Birkenhead). Intermediate stations at Hamilton Square and Central.

On this page an interior view of Hamilton Square station and opposite four 'Mersey Railway' scenes, starting with the booking hall there. More posing accompanies the illustration of MR No. 6 Fox at Birkenhead Central station. The lower two views depict, left, a rebodied Mersey Railway BSO at Birkenhead North in September 1956 and, right, a Class 503 unit at Rock Ferry in August 1985.

1888	2 Feb	Branch to Birkenhead Park opened.
1891	15 Jun	Green Lane to Rock Ferry extension opened.
1892	11 Jan	Extension to Liverpool Central opened.
1900		Mersey Railway Electrification Act passed.
1903	3 May	Last steam service. Electric service commenced.
1938	14 Mar	Through running of electric trains between Mersey Railway and former Wirral Railway; Mersey Railway took over the Liverpool to New Brighton services.
1948	1 Jan	Mersey Railway became part of British Railways.
1971	Feb	Work on the Liverpool Loop commenced.
1975	18 Jul	Liverpool Central Low Level closed.
1977	9 May	Liverpool Loop, and new junction at Hamilton Square, opened.
1978	25 Oct	Official opening of the Liverpool Loop by HM the Queen.

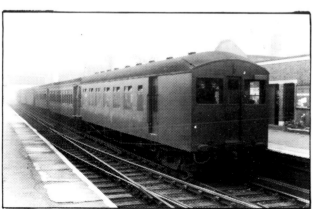

Birkenhead's Dockland

A complex network of running lines, goods sheds and sidings evolved over the years from 1847 when the railway first gained access to Birkenhead's docks. Numerous firms built their own private sidings and were responsible for their own shunting, often using horses or cables attached to capstans. Some of the larger concerns, such as Vernon & Sons or Paul Brothers, the millers, possessed more extensive systems and generated sufficient traffic to warrant purchasing their own locomotives. However for the smaller firms this was not an economic proposition and to serve their needs there arose various contractors operating fleets of small shunting locomotives. These contractors included William Lee of Seacombe, and Joseph Perrin & Son, and Rea Ltd., of Birkenhead. The last of these was also responsible for shunting at the Monks Ferry coal wharf where the Mersey steam tugs were coaled. The locomotives of all of the concerns were commonly seen at work, crossing the dock bridges, shunting the quaysides and being serviced outside their respective locomotive sheds.

The decline of the private shunting contractors was evident by the time of the Second World War. Two factors contributed to this: firstly the general decrease in the volume of traffic using the docks and secondly the decision of British Railways to operate their own fleet of dock locomotives. These included both steam and, later, diesel types. The last of the contractors' steam locomotives disappeared from the scene in the 1960s as they were sold or scrapped. Today the few surviving diesels find little employment and generally have their cabs boarded up, though the recent resurgence in coal traffic has provided some grounds for future optimism.

Cheshire, used in the docks for some 50 years, stands outside the locomotive shed of haulier William J. Lee.

A variety of shunting locomotives was provided by the main line companies for dock duties. The Great Western Railway employed a variety of pannier tanks fitted with warning bells, whilst the LMS often used ageing saddle tanks of LNWR origin. In the early British Railways days these were replaced by the Kitson-built 0-4-0 saddle tanks and the 2F 0-6-0 tanks and later still by a class of 204 hp diesel mechanical shunters from Hudswell Clarke. LNER motive power was provided from Bidston shed including Sentinel 0-4-0s and in the later years J94 'Austerity' saddle tanks. Today a solitary Class 03 diesel shunter generally suffices.

The availability of large dockside and floating cranes meant that Birkenhead Docks were often used by engineering concerns for the export of large items. Thus it was that locomotive products of Messrs. Nasmyth Wilson, Kitson and Beyer Peacock could be seen from time to time on the quaysides, destined for East Africa,

India or South America. Coaches too, were exported this way.

As the decade of the 1980s entered its second half the future of Birkenhead's dockland railways stood uncertain. The noise and bustle of former years is unlikely to return to dispel the air of decay which pervades the dockland area. The solitary shunter waits for work and the withdrawn electric units, stored in the Cavendish sidings, suffered from the combined effects of vandals and the elements before succumbing to the cutter's torch. Only infrequent dmu movements, grain trains and occasional railtours disturb the litter at the trackside.

Bidston iron ore dock in 1985 with coal hoppers being loaded for mgr movement to Fidlers Ferry.

The 'twin steam' illustration top left features a Sentinel steam wagon and saddle tank locomotive Homepride outside the Homepride warehouse in 1955. To its right appears the massive bulk of the Cheshire Lines Committee's warehouse as it appeared in 1975. The lower views feature shunting scenes on the dockland lines where the sharp curves necessitated short locomotives. Although photographed after nationalisation, both LMS 27528 and LNER 8207 still carry the liveries of their former companies.

In the illustration top left a pair of Vulcan-built Pacifics for the Great India Peninsular Railway rest on the dockside before their long ocean voyage. The date is 14 June 1930. The 0-4-0 well tank on the right, formerly used on the Liverpool Overhead Railway, worked at the Monks Ferry tugboat coaling wharf. The more recent scenes below show, left, Pegasus moving a rake of hoppers for the flour mills in November 1980 and, right, the Cavendish Sidings resting place for displaced Class 503 Merseyrail emus.

A dock shunter in disgrace. Perrin *appears to have found a new route between the granite setts. Such incidents could cause huge hold-ups as both road and rail traffic shared the right of way across the dock bridges. The locomotive was owned by the contractors of the same name.*

The Industrial Scene

Major civil engineering works such as the building of docks, canals, tunnels and railways inevitably involve the transport of plant and materials to, and spoil from, the main construction sites. Thus it was in the Wirral that various temporary, yet often extensive, contractors' rail systems were laid. Amongst these, and to illustrate their diversity, were the tracks laid by Price and Reeves during the works associated with the quadrupling · of the Birkenhead to Chester line in the early 1900s, the system laid by Nuttalls during the Mersey Tunnel construction contracts, and the network that Perrys built to aid the Bromborough Dock construction in the 1920s.

A second type of industrial line occurs when a manufacturing concern evolves a need to transport large quantities of either raw materials or finished products to or from a main line rail link. Examples of this in Wirral include the extensive Lever Brothers system at Port Sunlight and Bromborough Dock or the line linking the Wirral Colleries with the West Kirby branch at Parkgate.

A third type of industrial line is the self-contained railway localised within a single concern designed for movement of materials purely within the works or factory limits. The railways associated with Moreton Brickworks or the Morgan Refractories at Neston (or even the horse-drawn Price's tramway) would fall into this category.

Industrial systems associated with dockland are dealt with separately.

The demand for powerful steam locomotives of short wheelbase (to cope with the sharp curves prevalent on many industrial systems) was answered by a variety of locomotive builders who specialised in this type. Various examples operated in Wirral from the works of such builders as Manning Wardle, Hawthorn Leslie, Andrew Barclay and Peckett. In later years diesel types superceded steam and examples from John Fowler and the Yorkshire Engine Company, amongst many others, found employment on private lines in Wirral.

On the various narrow gauge systems a similar diversity of locomotive type existed, together with a plethora of wagon types.

The rail systems themselves were of a great variety of form, from lines of a temporary or even portable nature to carefully engineered lines laid to mainline standards. The Lever Brothers system boasted passenger trains for its workmen and even boasted a 'Royal train' for the visit of King George and Queen Mary!

On the previous page Queen Mary *is being prepared for the day's duties at the locomotive shed inside Lever Brothers Port Sunlight factory. Her workplace is pictured on this page in a panoramic view embracing 'internal user' wagons, Palvans (designed for palletised loads of soap traffic), tank wagons, a crane, and the 0-6-0 Bagnall* Montgomery of Alamein, *the most powerful unit in Levers' fleet. The main line to Bromborough Dock is in the background.*

On the opposite page are typical industrial steam and diesel machines, the former at work on the promenade extension at New Brighton in 1937 and the latter at the now-closed Mollington oil sidings with a modern BP tank in 1967.

These scenes show construction work on the Bromborough Docks location in the 1920s, a steam navvy at work loading to side tipping wagons and diminutive 1891 Hunslet 522 on the East River Wall site.

Between July 1959 and February 1960 Norwest Construction Ltd laid a pipeline from Spital Sewage Treatment Works to Eastham along the Dibbin Valley. The 4-wheel diesel machines are seen here in use with flat and tipping wagons.

During 1956 diesel shunters took over the steam duties at Port Sunlight. The lower view depicts a line of Barclay machines and the upper view the powerful Montomery of Alamein.

Wirral's Railways Today

For Wirral's railways the mid 1980s were years of nostalgia, change and progress. They were years for looking back and to the future.

1985 saw the demise of the Class 503 electric multiple units. These 'old-faithfuls', the first members of which were introduced by the LMS before the start of the Second World War, were added to in the mid-1950s. The oldest members were thus approaching 50 years of age when withdrawn from service. Crowds turned out in salute when a final railtour was organised in April. Two trains, including one of the original batch, made a complete tour of the electrified Merseyrail network. Though much loved by the railway enthusiast fraternity they were becoming rough-riding and less than popular with many of the travelling public. In their place came the Class 508 electric units transferred from the Southern Region of British Rail. Though not brand new these units introduced a new standard of airiness and comfort to the Wirral lines.

The end of September 1985 saw the extension of the electrified system from Rock Ferry to Hooton and the opening of a new station, Bromborough Rake, between Spital and Bromborough. Various essential safety measures were introduced in connection with the electrification. The entire 'built-up' section of the route was protected by means of 6 foot palisade fencing, whilst elsewhere much of the route was upgraded with mesh fencing. A vigorous campaign involving the local media was conducted to emphasize the potential hazards of the live rails both to children regarding the track as a playground and to adults used to taking short cuts across the line. Special rail patrols have been mounted to catch those trespassing onto the trackbed.

To coincide with the extension of the electrification to Hooton British Rail gradually introduced new class

A Class 508 set approaches Bromborough Rake from Bromborough in November 1985.

142 'Pacer' units on the Chester-Hooton-Helsby service. This service now operates with a 30-minute frequency throughout the day between Hooton and Chester with a five- or six-minute cross platform interchange time at Hooton onto the Merseyrail electrics. The Helsby line enjoys a 60-minute frequency with additional trains doubling the frequency at peak periods.

Excellent publicity advertising the even-interval service, the Zone and Saveaway tickets and the greater passenger comfort has produced a dramatic upsurge in passenger traffic. British Rail and the Merseyrail Passenger Transport Executive together forecast that passenger journeys to Liverpool would increase by a factor of 1.7 after an initial three-year 'settling-in' period. In practice this figure was achieved just two weeks after the service was introduced! At individual stations the factor was even larger! At Bebington the October figure

was 2.67 times that of March whilst at Port Sunlight it was 2.91 times higher. Even at the new Bromborough Rake station the number of Liverpool-bound passengers reached 2501 per week, only a fraction short of the 2550 ultimately expected! A success story indeed!

On the West Kirby and New Brighton branches there is an even-interval service of four trains per hour. On the first of these lines the new station at Town Meadow (between Moreton and Meols) has been agreed in principle though implementation awaits the completion of housing developments by private developers. Leasowe has become the station for a peak-hour bus interchange service. A 15 minute frequency of

Class 47 Total Energy *positions 70 tonne oil tankers at the discharge terminal at Van den Bergh's Bromborough factory. This was the first train of hot edible oil to arrive from the Purfleet factory (13 May 1986).*

buses provides commuter links for the Seacombe Estate and Upton with Liverpool trains during both morning and evening peak times.

Although the introduction of Class 142 'Pacer' trains to the Bidston-Shotton-Wrexham line has produced improved passenger standards the line does not receive financial support from the MPTE and therefore does not benefit fully from the comprehensive 'Merseyrail' advertising. Indeed the express bus services from Heswall to Liverpool compete with the trains for the commuter traffic. However various local timetables and leaflets refer to Bidston as the interchange point for the mid-Wirral line even though individual train times

Interchange at Hooton with electric and diesel multiple units in November 1985. Electric set 508 129 prepares to depart for Liverpool having transferred its passengers to the 2-car dmu bound for Chester.

are not always shown. The basic service is hourly throughout the day in each direction.

After years of gradual decline the freight side of Wirral's rail operations received a welcome, albeit temporary, uplift when, in the autumn of 1985, Bidston Dock came into use for the unloading of imported coal destined for the Fidlers Ferry power station near Warrington. The loaded trains were composed of merry-go-round hoppers, marshalled at the dockside by the diesel shunters of Rea's, the contractors, which were transferred from their site of repose at Duke Street for the purpose. The trains were hauled generally by Class 47 diesel locomotives from Bidston Dock by way of Birkenhead North, Canning Street North, Helsby and Arpley to Fidlers Ferry. Three departures took place each weekday with paths between Rock Ferry and Hooton being slotted into the frequent electric multiple

A Class 142 'Pacer' passes through Leighton, between Heswall Hills and Neston, on a Bidston to Wrexham service in 1985.

unit service. Further freight developments took place from May 1986 when Speedlink Distribution won a major ten-year contract to move edible oil between the Van den Bergh & Jurgens plants at Purfleet in Essex and Bromborough. The hot edible oil, transported in bogie tankers of 102 tonnes laden weight, will supply the Bromborough factory with its main raw materials for margarine manufacture. Bromborough is reached via Port Sunlight Sidings. The service consists of four trains per week.

Apart from these trains the freight service is somewhat sparse, with occasional grain wagons for dockland firms and permanent way trains being the principal traffic. It was thus inevitable that the mid-1980s should see the final closure of Birkenhead's Mollington Street locomotive depot, the responsibility for the routine maintenance of the few remaining dock shunters being transferred to Birkenhead North Depot.

Two items of nostalgia can complete this brief portrait of the 1980s Wirral railscene. Firstly, one of Birkenhead's Class 03 shunters which completed its journey from North Depot to Swindon via Crewe and Bescot was destined to become the last locomotive to be given a full overhaul at the former Great Western Railway works before their closure. How nice it would have been if it could have returned to Wirral resplendent in lined green livery to commemorate the severance of links between Birkenhead and the GWR! Secondly, North Depot itself was responsible for the refurbishing and repainting into a version of LMS maroon of the last surviving Class 503 unit. This formed the 'VIP' train conveying civic dignitaries to open the newly electrified Hooton extension. Additionally it provided unusual motive power for a series of pre-Christmas 'Shoppers Specials' and proved to be a major attraction at the Merseyrail Centenary Celebrations.

A

Portrait

of

Wirral's Railways

The B.R. Era

On page 65 a Class 508 is pictured at Bromborough Rake with a Rock Ferry train. Opposite is a more traditional scene, acting as a reminder that for nearly 20 years the nationalised railway system depended on steam traction. It features 4-6-0 No. 6859 Yiewsley Grange *of Birkenhead depot approaching Chester with a semi-fast from the Wirral in the 1950s. Then came the diesels, making familiar scenes like the one on this page in which a Hooton-bound dmu crosses the central span of Mollington Viaduct over the Shropshire Union Canal.*

Typifying BR's trainload freight activity, the view on this page shows a Class 47 passing through Port Sunlight in November 1985 with the 1300 Bidston Dock to Fiddlers Ferry block coal train.

The six scenes on the page opposite depict:

Top left – a dmu passing through Spital in 1984, with the third rail already laid for electrification.

Top right – a Wrexham-bound dmu passing the site of the former Burton Point station.

Centre left – under-employed docks shunter 03 162 standing at Duke Street in 1984.

Centre right – a Class 508 set entering Hoylake past traditional Wirral Railway signal box and crossing gates.

Bottom left – a train entering Bidston to collect Mid-Wirral passengers who have alighted from a Wrexham-bound dmu.

Bottom right – a New Brighton departure photographed from the site of the former rail connection for the sea wall extension of the 1930s.

A Class 501 unit enters Birkenhead North in November 1985. This is a former London District 3-car set with centre coach removed and converted to a Sandite unit.

Bibliography

G. Dow	The Great Central Railway (Vols. I-III) (1962; Ian Allan).
J.W. Gahan	The Line Beneath the Liners (1983; Countyvise/Avon-AngliA).
J.W. Gahan	Steel Wheels to Deeside (1983; Countyvise/Avon AngliA).
R.P. Griffiths	The Cheshire Lines Railway (1958; Oakwood Press).
C. Highet	The Wirral Railway (1961; Oakwood Press).
C. Highet	All Steamed Up (1975; Oxford Publishing Co.).
G.O. Holt	The North West (A Regional History of the Railways of Great Britain) (1978; David & Charles).
R.C. Jermy	The Storeton Tramway (1981; Countyvise/Avon AngliA).
M.D. Lister	The Railways of Port Sunlight and Bromborough Port (1980; Oakwood Press).
E.T. MacDermot	History of the Great Western Railway (1927; Ian Allan).
J. Marshall	Forgotten Railways of North West England (1981; David & Charles).
G.W. Parkin	The Mersey Railway (1961; Oakwood Press).
S.D. Wainwright	Rails to North Wales (1978; Ian Allan).
Merseyside Railway History Group	The Hooton to West Kirby Branch Line and The Wirral Way. (1982; Metropolitan Borough of Wirral).
Industrial Railway Society	Industrial Locomotives of Cheshire, Shropshire and Herefordshire (1977; IRS).
Railway Development Society	Cheshire and North Wales by Rail (1986; RDS).

Acknowledgements

The illustrations in this book are either from the author's collection or have kindly been supplied by the following: Birkenhead Library Collection (page 11), V.J. Bradley (57, 59), G. Earl (26), Ellesmere Port Library Collection (10), R. Fell (53), the late N. Forbes (52), R. Gaulder (18, 41, 42), G.D. Hawkins (40), Heyday Publishing (15, 44) Lens of Sutton (16, 48), M.D. Lister (26), B. Mathews (27), R. Miller (11, 14, 52), C. Millington (40, 53, 54), N. Parker (19, 22), G. Parry Collection (6, 38), J. Peden (20, 21, 37), Mrs Peers Collection (12), the late G.H. Platt (46), Real Photographs (32, 34, 45, 49), J. Ryan Collection (49), B.D. Stoyel (50, 57), H. Townley (16, 30, 38, 60), UML Ltd (14, 55, 56, 58, 60), Van den Bergh & Jurgens (62), I. Vaughan (9, 13, 31, 36, 39, 46, 66), J. Ward (19, 35, 37) and G.V. Winchester (53).

OTHER TITLES FROM
Countyvise

Local History
Birkenhead Priory £1.80
The Spire is Rising £1.95
Sidelights on Tranmere £2.95
The Search for Old Wirral £9.95
Birkenhead Park £1.40
A Guide to Merseyside's Industrial Past £1.95
Neston and Parkgate £2.00

Local Shipping Titles
Sail on the Mersey £1.95
The Mersey at Work — Ferries £1.40
Ghost Ships on the Mersey £1.40
Ferries Forever £3.50
The Liners of Liverpool – *Part 1* £2.95

Local Railway Titles
Seventeen Stations to Dingle £2.95
The Line Beneath the Liners £2.95
Steel Wheels to Deeside £2.95
Seaport to Seaside £4.25
The Storeton Tramway £2.20
Northern Rail Heritage £1.95

History with Humour
The One-Eyed City £2.95
Hard Knocks £3.95

Other Titles
Speak through the Earthquake, Wind & Fire £3.95
It's Me, O Lord £0.40
Companion to the Fylde £1.75

RAILWAY ITEMS FROM
AVONANGLIA

Postcards
InterCity 21st anniversary set of 8 full colour train postcards, £1.50
Rail Photo Print — 2 commemorative sets of period railways scenes, each of 8 duotone postcards, £1.40 per set.
BRP Railway Poster postcards, selection of 16 colourful poster subjects, £2.75.

Posters
Reprints of GWR/WR posters (choice of Oxford, St. Pauls, Barmouth, St Ives or Tower and Tower Bridge), £4.50 each plus £1 postage.
Mini posters (A4 size), selection of 4 railway poster subjects, ideal for framing, £2.95

Books
Oxford-Hereford Line, £1.75
The Severn Tunnel, £2.75
Railway of Central & West Wales, £1.95
LMS & GWR Jt. Sectional Appendix (Birkenhead/Chester/Shrewsbury/Hereford area), £4.25
Seventeen Stations to Dingle, £2.95
Line Beneath the Liners, £2.95
Steel Wheels to Deeside, £2.95
Seaport to Seaside, £4.25
All Change at Crewe, £1.75
Rocket 150: Liverpool & Manchester Rly, £2.40
Northern Rail Heritage, £1.95

Other Items
Railway Letter Stamps, 4 x GWR150 issue, £2.75
GWR Magazine Reprints, including 150 page 1935 Centenary Number, £4.95

Send for our full lists. Orders for above items to address below, adding 10% for postage on orders below £5.

Avon-AngliA Publications & Services, Annesley House, 21 Southside, Weston-super-Mare BS23 2QU.